Cenotaph

Cenotaph

Selected Poems by
Dan Carleton

Copyright © 2022 Daniel Webster Carleton
ggearinc@yahoo.com
www.webstervoice.com

ISBN 979-8-218-08851-4

Library of Congress Control Number: 2022920058

Published in Detroit, Michigan, United States of America

First Printing, 2022

To all of my grandchildren, even the unborn

Contents

Acknowledgments

Thank you to my sisters Nancy and Shelley for help with putting this book together and to Lee Pennington and Don Bunka for help with the baffling world of information technology. Also thanks to my helpers at Tell Tell Poetry.

Cenotaph

Cenotaph

I do not want to fill a tomb when I die
I want a poem as my cenotaph
Perhaps this poem, maybe another
A poem from life about death
A paradox
A bold statement
A sweeping statement to leave instead of a stone tomb
I want to fly away in death,
And leave an empty grave
Fly up into the galaxies
Fly past Planet Nine
Glancing over my spirit's shoulder at the blue marble
That I am leaving behind to go
Beyond sunlight into the depths of the universe
Among the trillions of types of beauty and terror
Around black holes,
Among supernovae
Among solar systems unlike ours
At the speed of thought
At the speed of love.
Leaving only this poem
This cenotaph

07/08/2022

I Find Myself

Every morning
I find myself
As someone else
I am becoming less capable
Less real
More afraid of dying
In spite of all the high falutin' philosophy I studied
In spite of all my agnostic beliefs
I grow old
I grow old
Wear the bottoms of my trousers rolled (Thanks Eliot)
And when I sit down at my crappy old desk
Which is becoming increasingly buried in stacks of papers
About which I cannot recall the provenance
In spite of my grasping determination
I feel the poems fading, disappearing before me
Yet baffled I stumble on undefeated by time or by myself
By myself I am
Attempting to write through the haze of long COVID
Attempting to write through the brain fog and exhaustion
Undefeated, foggy, lonely I struggle to write on.
Right on

05/11/2022

Midnight Ramble

It's midnight on some late winter night or other
And I am awake and sleep is hard to find.
I have hunted in every corner of my mind.
Through the cerebral cortex with gun and camera
Searching for poems
Searching for facts that will soothe my health driven panic.
My doctor says it is nothing to worry about.
Sure, he's not worried, it ain't his death.

And yet, as a long COVID patient
I don't feel very patient.
Four months of exhaustion, brain fog, and imbalance
And now, the cardiology consult.
The sticky squares on my chest
Sliding into that scary tube
Nurse Ratchett ordering me to be still and not move,
Which prompts me to ask which of those she wants
Which prompts an exasperated snort
And finally finished I go down the hall to the other office
To get my heart monitor "installed"
Which prompts visions of jack hammers and screw drivers
And turns out to be almost painless.

And now, finally at home I can almost relax
Almost

03/16/2022

Where I Come From

Now I know where I come from.
I come from water.
Water that many say came from the sky
On comets or meteorites
To fill the oceans
To cool the volcanic stone
Water where I lived a long nine months inside my mother
Water that nourishes the plants I eat.
Water in which kelp and lobsters grow.
I come from family
A family of artists
Mom's piano
Dad's writings and flowers
Shelley's violin and photos
Nancy's lovely voice
My 'cello and poems
I come from summers in the Maine woods, with mosquitos.
Swimming in the frigid water 'til my lips turned blue.
Searching tide pools for living treasures
Going to church on Sunday evening
In the old blue church
Where stained glass Jesus smiled up toward heaven.
Where Mom played the old pump organ
And we sang tonelessly to
"In the Garden"
"The Old Rugged Cross" and
"Let the Lower Lights Be Burning"

My life is lesser now.
Dimmed by loss of loves and passing years
My favorite stuffed animal is lost for more than sixty years
And all my pets have died or gotten lost
My house is sad and empty now

And yet, I still do not want to return to water.
Not yet.
I wish to know more
Even if more tells of loss and sad and empty houses.
Of loneliness

01/17/22

Mabel Doring

In one of my earliest memories at three years old
Three years old
I am falling
Backwards
Off a rickety and Northern Michigan dock
Brown water closing over my face
As I stare up at blue.
Mom watches, screaming in terror frozen in terror
As Mabel dives into the brown lake water
And saves my life.
Thinking of what I would have missed without her
All the wonderful food
The divorces
The great sex
The herpes
The love
The hate
The unwritten poems
The loneliness
My life
My death
A lot to miss when you think about it...
Thanks Mabel

12/26/2021

T-shirts

With apologies to W.Shakespeare

I bought the other day two new t-shirts.
I was at the truck stop, just buying gas
And getting a bottle of water to ease my throat
And walking past a display of tough guy trucker clothes
I came upon a plain t-shirt, with pocket
Army green
Extra large
Extra green
Two for ten bucks.
After I got them home
A good wash
A tumble dry
And now, I am thinking of when to pull one of them out
From among the dress shirts and suits and ties and braces
And wear it.
I'll have to pick one of them
I think tomorrow will be just the day.
For me to creep in this petty pace
Until the last syllable of recorded time
And wear the damned t-shirt already
The President Walenski look alike t-shirt

03/15/2022

Intimate

Tall and sexy
A big black woman
She leans in, liquid brown eyes focused entirely on me
Focused on my pale blue eyes
My pale white skin
My quivering upper lip.
She studies my ears.
She studies my veiny hands and forearms.
Caresses my scalp
Massages my rigid neck and tips my chair back.
Concentrating, she leans over, pressing her breast
To my shoulder to brush something off my thigh.
And once the steaming heat is cooled
I pay for the haircut and walk into the freezing morning
Unsatisfied

02/01/2019

The Ugly Truckling

Squatting in my driveway like a toad on a lily pad
This old truck fits me
Like that old flannel shirt with holes in the elbows,
Her driver's seat
Comfortable, familiar, fits my butt
Like my old reading chair in the living room
She squats
Rusty, full of holes, bumperless,
Her tailgate held up by a dozen bungee cords
She squats.
Her ugly dependability manifest,
Nearly forgotten in its everydayness
We are like a couple married seventy years
Knowing each other
Beautifully

I sit at my desk
Slightly hunched, tired and sore of foot
This poem fits me like a familiar old sweatshirt.
It speaks of the comfortable,
Like my aloneness, a comfortable loneliness.
I am dented, worn, broken of shoulder and knee
Weary of the requirements of life;
Yet this poem is looking for tomorrow's next challenge.
Looking back on old challenges
Rhetoric teaching
Gear machining
Lobster fishing
Trucking
And so many other ings
I am a walking breathing gerund

Looking for
A challenge of subject
A new perspective
A perfect rhythm
A way to resee my aging self
To keep the poems flowing for one more day.

12/09/2021

The Bottom Step

Waiting for the dryer I see
My fancy bicycle, tires flat
My tool boxes, old and dented and scratched
Some are new and plastic, modern
That strange almost finished room behind the sinks
Fluorescent tubes humming, flashing blue white
The old bedstead that Dad carved with pineapple corners
And boxes, so goddamned many boxes, plastic, cardboard
An old dresser scratched with missing drawers.
The others filled with forgotten blankets, old nuts and bolts
Bags full of old chemicals
A sagging shelf of old machineries handbooks
And shirts, the ones that I should have donated years ago
The ones I promise myself I will donate next
Jackets and slacks hang on pipes

And suddenly I am back at college
Where I lived in a buddy's basement
With a waterbed and hundreds of books
Jackets and slacks hung on pipes.
When it rained, a stream ran right through my room
From the eastern wall to the floor drain next to the shower.
The shower that was only feet from the waterbed
The shower that had no stall or even a curtain
The shower under which I spent pleasurable hours
In showers with lovers.
Basement life has treated me well indeed.

02/02/2022

Plants

Face it, my house plants intimidate me.
Juicy inside
And they're green.
I always handle them with exaggerated care.
Sometimes I skip the watering
Just to show me who's boss;
But I have three that have managed to survive the
Neglect to which I have subjected them.
The Amaryllis continues to be green.
The Christmas cactus that bloomed for Valentine's Day,
Again for Thanksgiving, no matter how holiday inaccurate
And one big succulent, refusing borders
Is spilling over the shelf on which it lives.
All of them are challenging me to put them down
But I refuse, no matter how creepy their challenges
To do their bidding.
They challenge me to cut them back
But for some reason I hesitate.
Except for the Cannabis
It has been stripped and stored in the freezer
For later use
Medication for
Intimidation

02/05/21

Boxing Day

On Boxing Day I gather them
Sadness, hate, love, disappointment, loneliness, apathy.
They hide beneath the sofa, among dust bunnies, behind the
   washer-dryer and in that curious drawer under the oven.
At the dog park they try to foil my efforts at control,
At the library they slither between bookshelves
At the gas station I catch them peeking from behind pumps.
Mercilessly, I box them up without wrapping, without ribbons,
   without tape, without styrofoam peanuts.
I put on gloves and pummel them with my best left hook, right
   cross combination until they lie on the canvas, panting with
   bloody exhaustion;
And yet they rise, undaunted, clinging to the ropes to fight again.

12/31/18

At A Glance

On a whim I open up my Spam folder
And find:
Penis growth secrets revealed
And
Instahard—How to control your manhood
And
Hot wife rides fifteen inch African beast
And
Squirtmaster: How to make a woman squirt
And
Sex Secrets: German sex industry penis ritual
And
Long and strong: Give your manhood a boost

The wisdom of our culture
The wisdom of this internet

06/03/2022

Warning

I went down to the basement.
I told myself it was for the laundry
The laundry that had been there for days
And a search that I had intended to do for weeks
For the perfect cord I needed
To fit the old shillelagh
That I found last year.
And as I was just a little tired
And didn't want to climb the steps just yet.
And there were tools that needed sorting
And a lovely bottom step on which to sit
And listen to NPR on the radio
That I just happened to bring along
Back when the laundry and the cord and the tool sorting were my goals
Before the radio warned me
Of that damned tornado.

06/26/21

By the Roadside

It lay in the break down lane
Brown, stirring slightly in the chilly wind
Splashed by the passing cars in the rain.
Moving slightly to attract perhaps attention?
Moving slightly to combat the chill?
Or to shake off the grime of the break down lane?
We will never know the thoughts of a discarded plastic bag.
We will never know the thoughts of the break down lane.
The earth will breathe without our analysis.
The galaxy will spin around itself for a time
Billions and billions of years
And we will never know what the galaxy thinks.
We shall just carry on living, thinking,
Dying

01/01/2022

The Rub

From: Yeats, Thomas, Eliot, and Shakespeare

At seventy-one and troubled years I am driving through green.
Cloud shadows, bushes, evergreens all
Blend
Move
Become
An undiscovered wilderness of silence
Unlike Yeats' country this IS a
Country for old men
Despite
The young in one another's arms.
I am whelmed by green
Teased by chartreuse and *tickled by the rub of love.*
Seduced by the closeness of color, by thoughts
Of land in the mountains above the Winooski River
Of land to build my house, my future, my *one bean row*, where
I can read in an easy chair, and *wear the bottoms of my trousers rolled:*
A place to live, a place to die, *perchance to dream.*

07/24/2019

20

Sunday Morning

with apologies to Wallace Stevens

Complacencies of the jockey shorts, and late
Beer and pizza in a sagging armchair.
No cockatoo, only a robin and a worm
No she, just me
Wondering if this life, bereft of joy is really worth it.
Worth waking in the dark of three
To the pounding of an IRS headache
Worth wondering from where the next dollar,
The next meal will come from.

Feeling the shame of skipping the cetology chapters
In Melville's masterpiece
The gutlessness of standing in front
Of the Anne Frank house
And turning instead to go to the City Five coffee house.
And never reading A Brief History of Time
Even though in college I carried it around like I was.
Masquerading as an alone person, while pretending
To not be lonely, and never to an infinitive split.

OK, I am waiting for someone to recognize my goodness
To see my soul for its' blameless blankness.
Waiting.

04/25/2022

Craig

We are sitting in my living room
Two old guys reminiscing about our lives since junior high.
Two days into this marathon of talking
Two days into our separate and woven intersecting thoughts
Two days since I arrived home to my old and lonely house
To find my friend of sixty years in the kitchen with a beer.
We spent a few delicious days exploring
Our minds
And all the important stuff
Cars
Women
Motorcycles
Beer
And now he is gone and
I remain
Alone
Lonely
But I will pretend.
I will soldier on.
Working
Writing
Hoping to find those missing years when inspiration flowed.

05/26/2022

Nuel Davis Visits Me

I am sitting in Vermilion County Jail
Trying not to go completely crazy
Trying to be tough enough
It isn't noisy
It isn't cold
It isn't even scary
Just lonely.
No one visits
No one cares
Woe is me.

And suddenly a surprise at the bars to my cage
My writing professor
Best selling author and mentor
Nuel Pharr Davis of Laurence and Oppenheimer fame
He chose to visit me in jail.

I am a mixture of embarrassment and awe
A mixture of gratitude and shame
Blame him for a lot of this poetry.
Blame Nuel for being a friend.
Blame Nuel for the forty mile drive to see me behind bars.

A friend in need

05/26/1969

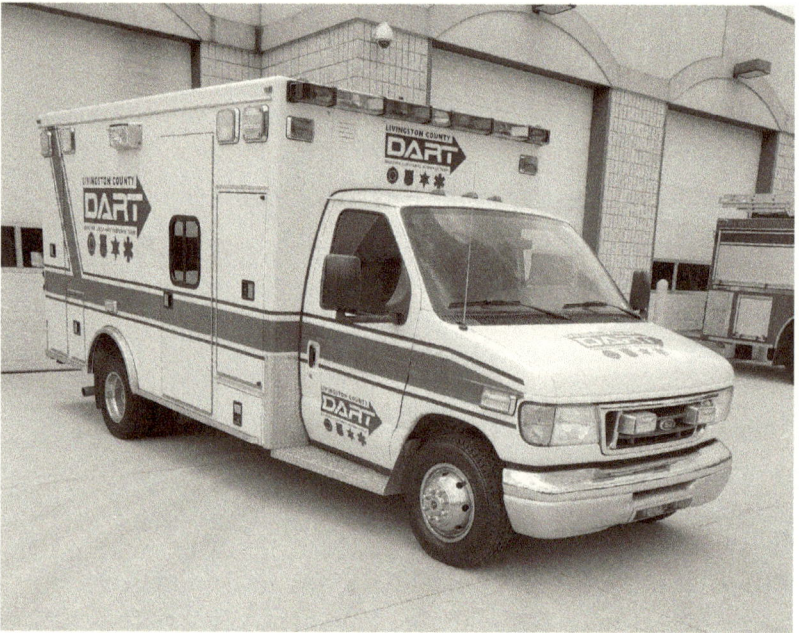

Ambulance

In my dream I am in an ambulance
And I am dreaming of an ambulance
I have been shot
In the arm, the upper arm
And I am dreaming of the bullet
S L O W motion
Gun to shoulder takes ten minutes
Flashing red light
Screaming
Wailing siren
Dark, icy woods flash with the red
Lights? Blood?
Death awaits
Or the accident
My BMW sliding off the road
All ribs broken
Both shoulders dislocated
Falling falling
Body broken, tumbled
Helicopter thumps
Lights flashing
Blood red,
Emergency red
ER doctor telling me he thinks I won't die
I Need to tell my kids I love them

06/11/2022

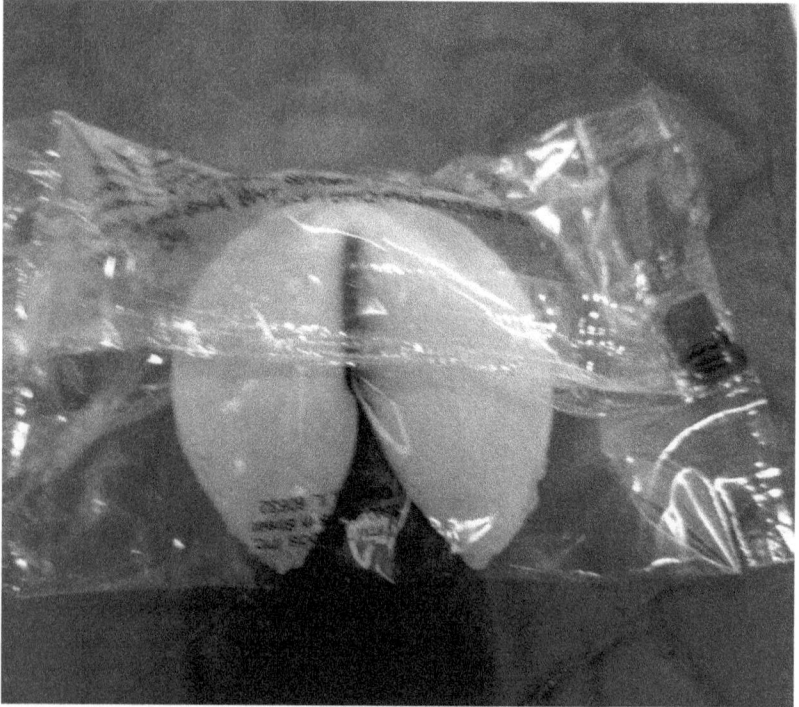

Fortunate

Stuffed with salted eggplant vegan style
And Sichuan fried green beans
We laugh at human failings
And criticize the internet and all social media
And at last we are full but continue to talk
Knowing we will at last head out to go home
Alone from each other
But soft!
The bill arrives carried on its' own private little tray
And there are two fortune cookies,
Created just to play the read it and add "in bed" to the end.
Randi opens hers first. "You will have good fortune tonight"
To which we both shout "In Bed" with gales of laughter.
I open mine.
I crumble the cookie.
The empty cookie
No fortune,
And we laugh an uncomfortable laugh
Which turns to a curious silence
An uncomfortable, almost spooky silence
No one takes fortunes in cookies seriously
Do we?

07/27/2022

Memory

I have a memory problem
I remember far too much.
I can sit remembering for hours
Remembering the hours and the minutes
My life can roll by like a black and white and nineteen twenties film
Or flash like the visual of the Enterprise going to warp speed
I am not another hyperthymesic Marilu Henner
Or Borges' fictional Funes the Memorius
But I am sometimes paralyzed by memories
Of the softness of fog
Of the sound of my Harley
Of the taste of beets
Of my bedroom curtains blowing in the sea breeze
Of the touch of a lover's hand.

Memory problems indeed

06/30/2022

Ace

My daughter, Caitlin has become someone.
Someone who has become with and through his name.
A pretty little girl with ribbons in her hair and dolls.
Playing the 'cello like her dad
Using her easy bake oven
To be like her old timey image of a mom.
Then to school with all the others
The neighbor girl who came to her birthday party
And noticed that our spoons didn't match
And the son of that basketball star who liked her in high school
And her little pal from next door who loved horror movies
And playing doctor with her girl friends
Learning to kiss and growing hair in strange places

And college, land of discovery,
LGBTQ discovery politics, where Caitlin became a discoverer
Becoming a tile setter, a woodworker, a teacher, then
Moving to Vermont, marrying Diana,
Teaching at Murray's Institute near New College
Starting to build houses, he became Ace,
Business owner, changeling, no ribbons,
Manager, hammer swinging builder, tile setter
And now that he's Ace,
He carried Yara in his womb
Made me proud grandpa, proud father, of
Ace

There's power in that name.
There's purpose in that name.
I am so damned proud of my kid

Caitlin McArleton has become
Ace McArleton and he will become
More
So much more.

03/11/2022

Grandma

With apologies to Dylan Thomas

I am five years old
And Daddy has brought me and Nancy and Shelley and Mom
To see his mother.
It has been a long drive in the old Buick
But I did get to ride on the back shelf,
Mostly I can see now, to keep me from fighting with my sisters.
A long ride because it is a ride no one wants to take
Particularly Daddy.
We stop in front of the "Rest Home"
God's Waiting Room.
This place is gigantic, prison like,
And we walk in the front door single file
Like prisoners to the firing squad.
Like students to detention
Family but separate.
My sensitive five year old nose,
Detecting disinfectant, urine and that special odor of institution
My nose causes me to hold back
Pulled along by my fear of being left alone
Pulled along by my big sister's hand
Held back by the smell
Held back by fear of Grandma
Who is old and scary and has false teeth and awful breath
And one of those hairy moles on her cheek
And who insists on hugging and fussing over all of us.
I am ashamed of my fear of her
I am ashamed of my fear of her age and her smell

I am ashamed that I have become her.
Old and alone in my room and smell.
Wanting so badly to see my grandkids

31

I am ashamed that my words have "forked no lightening"
Old and lonely and needy.
I am simply a shame.

02/26/2022

Burning Leaves

To G.M.Hopkins

Odors like memory anchors.
The smell of Hopkins' autumn leaf mold brings me back
To childhood in Illinois.
We'd rake the lovely autumn maple leaves into the street
And set fire to the piles
Set fire to the pastel and lovely piles
Set fire to them and create a thick and acrid smoke
That lingered in my clothes all day
That lingers in my mind's nose today.

Wrong for living things and wrong for the Earth, but
I'd would love to go back to the piles and the play and
My mom ringing the bell on the porch of the old house
On Garfield Street. The old stucco house where she is
Ringing the bell to tell us to come home to dinner
Ringing the bell to tell me to come back to 1956.

Return with me now to the day
When Jackie Gleason was hilarious when he yelled,
"To the moon Alice"
And Lucy messed up Ricky's stardom with her
Wacky feminine antics.
And Amos and Andy were those amusing Negroes.
"Holy Mackerel there Andy"
I can still smell the burning humor.

12/08/2021

33

Celene

Mom brings me to the garret room to see her mother.
And I look up at the ancient wrinkled face
Surrounded by a halo of white hair.
She is sitting in an ancient chaise lounge, painted white
Surrounded by light green pillows.
Her ancient wrinkled face lights with delight when she sees me
Her little two year old grandchild.
And we begin our game.
Although a stroke has taken her words,
And I do not have many of my own
We communicate with eyes and smiles and giggles.
Let the games begin.
I run to her and place my tiny hands on the green cushion.
Smiling her amazing smile, she covers my hands with hers.
I can feel her love even through the papery skin.
I pull away and run to Mom whose tears I do not notice.
And I pull away from Mom to run back
To the paper white and ancient woman
On the painted white and ancient chaise
My tiny hands are covered by her ancient papery bony hands
And our eyes meet and giggles explode and I pull away
To run back to Mom our speechless game.
It is my earliest memory.
I play my own version of it today with equal delight
With my grandkids.
I am become my grandmother,
Approaching our fate together.

02/26/2022

Mom

The steamship Cunard Princess started it all.
In 1921 after my grandfather died
Mom won a grand prize for piano performance
That sent her and her mom and her sister to Paris for a year
So Mom could study piano with Nadia Boulanger.
But a lone woman traveling with two daughters
Was just not done in '21
So Robert came along to Europe on the Cunard Princess
Handsome, intelligent, charming,
Robert was a poet.
In his twenties, he was a crush magnet for 15year old Mom.
She didn't forget.
Didn't forget piano
Or poetry
Or Robert
And later, married to my dad,
With three kids,
She never forgot.

II.

Evenings in bed
Mom read to me
The poems of Donne and Whitman
Until sleep overtook me.
I see her now, slight and grey, reading to my sleeping bedroom.
Poems were my ambien
Poems were the arms of Morpheus
Poems are now my heroin,
My addiction for more than sixty-five years
From grade school
To high school

To college
To lobster fishing
To gear machining
To now

I have written down my words
On a compact typewriter in my college dorm
On the backs of envelopes while I drove
In notebooks on airplanes
In Chinese hotel rooms on the free notepads
And today on this computer.

Haikus
Sonnets
Parodies of Shakespeare and Milton
A shape poem or two.
Always without a goal in mind…
Just writing.
And finally I have published a book of this stuff.
I never intended to do this.
Didn't much care to publish
I was just writing.
And now, I want to give poetry to my children, grandkids
My friends and colleagues.
To give them some pieces of me, some pieces of mom.

12/20/1999
04/03/2022

Child's Play

Quietly I daydream of my grandson Liam
Lanky fast impulsive Liam
As he runs the pitch
He is the fastest of them
Not aggressive
But skilled and swift
Swift and skilled

And then I attend the play
Liam is the lead.
Liam is the captain of the ship
Liam is my hero

And then the whole family goes to lunch

Dashiell
Lives up to his nickname: Dash
This kid can get his way around the pitch.
He is aggressive and skilled and promised his teacher
That he will be a big soccer star someday
And bring money to family.
After his game
We go to lunch.

04/20/2022

Yara

I can see her now
Kneeling, concentration writ large on her small face
At school
Not thinking of me
Or Papa
Or Mama
Or baby Elio.
She is concentrating on objects: multi hued, geometric.
Spread out on the floor before her.
As if rolled misshapen dice
Rolled for only her
Her concentration lovely
Her growing self evidence evident.
She is as much the future as I am the past
Thrilling

04/22/2022

Lake Lola Montez

High in the High Sierras
We are camping in the High Sierras
Ace and I
I came out here to visit after her college graduation
She was working in the city
So we came to the country
To spend time together and found this lake
Untouched and perfect
With clear water.
And what does a person do when they find a lake?
Swim of course
In water turned brown by the pines along the shore
We swim with tiny blue fishes that dart before us
Tiny darting gems by the thousands

I see the tiny gems transformed to the herring schools
That we pumped from the purse seine on Matinicus
Silver knives as long as your hand
Ten thousand bushels of silver knives
Sardines, or lobster bait, or just fillets for smoking or dinner

Celebration gems and silver
A graduation present indeed

05/18/2022

The Cliff Dwellers

Sitting on the balcony at my father's club
Facing the lions at the Art Institute nine stories below
Across LaSalle Street.
We sip lemonade and talk
Mom and Dad and two of us three kids
It's early on a Thursday evening
And this is our weekly night
To attend the Chicago Symphony Orchestra.
Time to suck up some culture.
Time to suck down a burger and fries while
Rochester, our regular waiter exchanges a few polite words
With Dad, about Socrates or some other boring stuff.
After dinner, we take the elevator down one story,
And are escorted to our seats.
We listen quietly to the first piece, and then a second,
And then Dad's head drops to his chest
And he begins to snore loudly.
Mom delivers an elbow to his ribs
Awakening him with a snort and a loud
"Just resting my eyes dear"
To add to Mom's mortification.
We ride home in the Buick in uncomfortable silence.

05/19/2022

CSO

Time to hear some serious music
Not that crap they play on the radio.
Time to see my 'cello teacher, who sits third 'cello
At the Chicago Symphony Orchestra.
I can see him right behind the first 'cello
Right at the edge of the stage
I watch him carefully
He sits ramrod straight
Behind the first 'cello at the edge of the stage.
The first 'cello is a drama king of the first order
It looks as if he is trying to saw his instrument in half
With his bow.
But not my teacher,
Not Alois Trnka
Ramrod straight
His regal movements playing the same notes as the drama king
I want everyone to know he is MY teacher.
At my weekly lesson in his basement
He is demanding, sometimes even a little mean
But once I played the intro to La Boheme without a mistake
And he reached into his pocket and gave me a quarter
He gave it to me with a flourish
I kept that quarter until I was forced to spend it on candy
Sad souvenier

05/20/2022

Ants

This morning I had had enough.
I found them crawling on my toothbrush.
Since I have killed so many creatures, mostly fish and lobsters
I can feel their detritus building on my soul
I really hate to do it;
But I went to the store, bought some ant baits
And put them out in my bathroom.
Ants, although they might be aunts as well, sisters to a queen
They should not be crawling on my toothbrush.
So I did it,
In spite of Queen Lizzie's Platinum Jubilee today
Take that, you arthropods!
You mirmidons
You hymenopterons

06/02/2022

My Neighbor

Black and white and not at all stealthy
He crosses the yard.
Crosses the brown and patchy lawn
Beautiful
Graceful
His tail waving like a medieval battle banner.
His pointy little head inspecting the ground
Stopping occasionally to gobble up some tasty morsel
Lifting his pointy little head to sniff the air.
There is a lot to sniff in the early spring air.
Salt on the driveway
Trees not yet budding out
Trash in fragrant overflowing cans
Tires on my rusty old truck
And me.
But he's not afraid of me.
Even though he sees me standing on the porch of the house.
He heads straight for me,
Not hurrying, still hunting tasty morsels
The skunk heads straight for me.
And disappears under the porch of my house:
Indeed his house.

03/01/2022

Mounted Head

My buddy walks me out through the back of the house
Into the vast winter corn field
He shows me the circle where he had found the deer.
Starved, struggled and frozen to death.
It had somehow gotten its' right front hoof
Caught in its' right front rack
And had fallen and struggled in a spinning circle
Until it died.
His dog found it
Dead in the winter cornfield
And his barking brought my buddy out
To this bizarre tableau.

Back in the house, I got to see the mounted head
A six point rack
With a hoof caught in the right side
A hell of a way to die.

02/26/2022

Rusty

I confess: I am an unabashed lover of squirrels.
Squirrels are smart
Squirrels are lightning fast
Squirrels can be trained to come when called
And damn it, they are just plain cute.
Squirrels have a prodigious memory for where their stuff is.
A squirrel can hide ten thousand acorns
And find ninety percent of them for winter food
And I can't find my car keys with any reliability.
And damn it, they are just plain cute.

When I was six
I had a stuffed squirrel named Rusty
I loved that squirrel with my innocent child's heart
I had to have him to sleep with me at night
And damn it, he was just plain cute.

Of course, I insisted on taking him to school with me
And I lost him on the way home, walking on Madison Street
From a school long gone
To a home no longer mine.
My parents were kind and helpful,
Walking the route to search as if looking for a lost diamond
They even bought me another one that looked like Rusty
But it was no good.
Even living squirrels can never replace Rusty
My love for him will never die and can never be replaced.
But there's a town named Longview Washington
That built tiny bridges over a busy highway
To save the squirrels that often gave their lives to cross.
High enough to let full sized semis pass under
Yet only wide enough to let a squirrel cross.
The townspeople had to scatter food on the tiny bridges

To trick the squirrels into safely crossing.
And once the first bridge proved successful
They built others to save their favorite little rodents.
Longview now has a squirrel festival in autumn
I plan to go for Rusty and me

04/01/22

Parakeet

Knowing that mom was lonely we thought to get her a pet.
She was ninety-eight years old
The gerontologist suggested a bird
Mom came along to the pet store.
And we got her the bird, the cage, the food and a book
She loved that bird
She talked to it.
She fed it
She was bird crazy
The bird would fly around her room
One day the bird went missing
We never found its' little corpse
Mom forgot after we took away the cage, the food, the book.
She settled on Animal Planet on the television.
Her mind was soon to fly away
And then her life
I was so angry
I am so angry.
That damned Parakeet

04/23/2022

Clydesdales

Stoned, we stumble down the quadrangle at the U of I
Ted and Chad and I
And finding the Stock Pavilion doors unlocked
We stumble in to get out of the rain and chilly wind.
The air is liquid
The air is humid with horse shit and hay
With mystery and moonlight
Liquid with heavy silence
Quiet as sleep
But we sense rather than hear
Horses
Lots of horses
Huge horses
The horses of Thor
Horses of all the gods of Asgard
And the big red wagon
Waiting to be pulled by these magnificent horses
Whinnying onto the fields of praise, (thanks Dylan)
Well, okay the football field
There in Champaign
Yet they stand there still as mountains, breathing gently
Breathing deeply
Still as buildings
Quiet as fish.
Powerful as eyesight
Clydesdales.
Mischief impossible, cleaned out by awe,
We sneak silently out
And stumble to the Turk's Head Ale House
In subdued and quiet wonder
Too stoned,
Too awed to talk,
Too whelmed to understand

What gods we have seen
What wonders we have witnessed.

10/10/1968

Kensington Metropark

Craig and I are sitting on a rough and worn and wooden bench
At the Kensington Metropark.
The greens and browns and yellows surround us
A benevolent fog of color
A buffet for the eyes
Talking idly about the weather
Joking about the rain gods and their fickle treatment
When, stalking down the path,
Noble
Brown
Red
Four feet tall
With golden eyes staring with empty intensity
Those spindly legs, three toed, black with backward knees.
This amazing bird walks right up to us
And asks for something.
But, not speaking Sand Hill Crane, we fail to understand.
But Craig reaches out to this strange and awkward bird
And for his lack of understanding
Receives a peck on the hand from that long bird beak.
So much for interspecies love

05/26/2022

Stink Bugs

These damned bugs are crawling in my kitchen
And they repulse me and piss me off
Yet when I kill them I feel like the ancient mariner
After the albatross fell
And perhaps the world is going to hell
Not because of my bug slaughtering;
But because it deserves to be there
I don't need to be clutching at the arm of a wedding guest
To tell my story of stink bug death.
I am not a weeping fool confessing to murder of a prostitute.
But this is the nature of our natures and nature
Creatures kill other creatures to survive
To be left alone
To save themselves
To save their offspring
Creatures kill
We kill.

05/23/2022

In Zurich

In a crowded cellar jazz club on November eleventh
Somewhere below the Niederdorf Strasse
I sit in the smoky air loving
Improvisational jazz and the anonymity of the crowd
But at last I give up, finishing my beer
And wander up to the street
Stopping to buy a wurst mit kraut from a street vendor
Who takes my hundred franc note for a two franc sausage.
And I sit at his rickety old table
The rickety old table with a book of matches under one leg.
A fix that fails to fix the ricketiness
Which I find somehow comforting in this country of perfection.
It is nearly midnight and the cobbled street is full of tourists.
Shops are open.
I bin the sausage wrapper and enter the rug merchant.
Oriental carpets hang on the walls, hang from the ceiling
And hang from wooden racks.
I feel swallowed by woolen beauty, like a cow in a squeeze
Like Jonah in the whale
An infant swaddled by carpets.
I turn and without a word go next door
To the Herren Mode shop and buy the wildest tie they have.
The joint next door to the Men's store sells nakedness
And the drinks are free if you pay the fifty franc cover.
A huge pinball parlor sets up a cacophony of dings and dongs
And the street tables are full at the Hotel Splendide
While inside at the piano bar they sing old Beatles tunes.
And couples shout at one another through the din.
Just one more beer at the Splendide, and
I stumble across the bridge and into the church.
The one called the Woman Church.
Its' stained glass windows by Marc Chagall,
Backlit at midnight by the lights of the city and the moon.

A stone's throw from the Woman Church is Pierre Cardin
And next to Pierre, the elegant old Hotel Zurich
And Rolex, Panera, Omega have shops in the twisted alleys
That climb the hills above the Limat River
And looking across the Limat to the opposite hill
I see the funicular descending from the Grand Hotel.

Recrossing the Limat, I am suddenly surrounded
Astounded
By dozens of crazily costumed knights, nobles, queens
Singing, dancing and playing flutes, tubas, guitars
To celebrate victory over Nazis, they throw candy, toys,

And finally I take a long walk up the hill toward Oerlikon
And another restless night in my tiny noisy room
At the Hotel Krone Unterstrasse
Listening to the trams in the street below.

In the morning I sit in the breakfast room at a small table
With the beatnik guy in the ascot
And the black fingernail polish
And the sandals with black socks.
And then catch the tram up the hill to Oerlikon, to work.

11/11/1997

In Shanghai

Jet lagged, sleepless I am riding on the Maglev
The miracle train that is traveling
At three hundred miles an hour
Toward downtown from the airport.
Faraday's magnets do their jobs
Making a ten mile long in-line motor.
I stare at the speed displayed over the entrance door.
Even though I could easily look out of the window
To see the blur of the run down apartments we are passing
At 300 miles an hour
Or are they passing us?
Ten minutes of incredible speed, and finally slowing
We arrive at the downtown station
I pass through the turnstile and buy a round trip ticket
To ride this wonderful train again.

And come back again to the noise and confusion of section Nine
Night clubs
Restaurants
Some business guy puking in a trash can
And the odor of fish from the nearby river.
Neon and noise
The cloudy midnight sky is lit by the city below.

03/15/2000

Airplane Food

Let me be the only person to celebrate airplane food.
Peanuts
Pretzels
Bischoff cinnamon cookies
Lifeless salads
Tiny tasteless bricks of hard cheese
Small plastic glasses of warm tomato juice
All have helped to break up my terror of riding eight miles high
In a tube as heavy as my house.
A tube traveling six hundred miles an hour
A tube that would make a mess on impact with the ground
And yet I know that

My death grip on the plastic arm rest
Is all that keeps this tube in the sky.
Along with my concentration
Along with my terror

Finally the crunch of the landing gear coming down
The jerk of the tires on the runway.
And I release the arm rests,
Stand up and shuffle down the aisle to escape.

02/17/2022

Halley's Comet II

(see Halley's Comet in Vol.1 pg 22)

Tom and I disembarked the Abel Tasman
On a warm and February morning in Hobart, Tasmania.
From the rented car we toured the big squarish island
Our guidebook showing us the largest pit mine on earth
And caves with glow worms and
We drove by botanic gardens and
On that warm and summer afternoon
We found ourselves at The Old Saloon, booked for the night
Got a table reserved for dinner
Which the proprietor found highly amusing
As we were the only guests
Ate dinner at the amusing table—
Huge and bloody steaks and French fries
And with dark approaching
Wandered out to sit on the porch and wait for full dark.

Full dark and we set out to drive until we saw no lights
No lights from towns or buildings or roads or boats.
Full dark indeed.
Our headlights shined off the blacktop
And after a time we came to an open field
An open field without a tree to be seen
And we stopped and walked into the field
Full dark and we had a view of the full sky
Without even a watt,
Without a jot of light pollution.
Full dark with the Southern Sky ablaze with stars
And centered overhead was Halley's Comet
Full dark as light as afternoon
Full dark as strange as ever

And as I and Tom stood transfixed by the sky show
The silent world passed by
Passed by as we stood transfixed
Until, exhausted by strangeness and wonder
We returned to the Old Saloon to sleep

07/10/2022

Frigid Fluids

I made four sets of gears for each of their machines
One for each corner.
I made them carefully of 4140 heat treated steel
Made them carefully on the Gleason gear generator.
And then I brought a sample down to Frigid Fluids
Near the Elevated tracks in deep Chicago.
The tracks whose plaster walls were painted with
The Goodbye Gallery
Extinct species depicted in bright and vibrant colors,
Wolly Mammoths, Aurochs, and the Carolina Parakeet
Lumber, graze and fly
Across the street from Frigid Fluids.
And the aroma of the Blommer Chocolate Company
Exotic as a Zoroastrian monastery
Comforting as chocolate cake on your tenth birthday.

Yet comfort is not on offer at Frigid Fluids.
I wait in the demonstration suite
Surrounded by their wares
Huge floor lamps
Fake oriental rugs
Stereo systems for playing Muzak to gatherings of folks
And when the shop foreman comes to get me,
Old and Polish, Chicago to the core
A grizzled four day beard
Greasy overalls hang off his shoulders
Like off a bent coat hanger
Breath like a swamp.
He grunts at me, refusing my handshake.
Gesturing to the open door, he leads me to the shop.
I hand over my carefully made bevel gears and
He grunts, and as I watch
Assembles them into the first of four corner housings:

Housings that hold the gears that turn the shafts
Housings that control the movement of the straps
Straps that hold the casket
On the Frigid Fluids Casket Lowering Device

He grins, yellow teeth dully reflecting the dim light
"You'll take your last ride on one of my machines"

Chocolate cake indeed.
Goodbye Gallery for certain

11/30/2011

Precision Mechanisms

A tube straightened to five microns per foot
A clip that holds eight cylinders.
The buffer tube
The delta ring
The ejection port cover
The ejection port cover hinge pin snap ring
And the ejection port cover pin
Ejection port cover spring

All work together to make the AR-15
So useful for chopping down trees
Or groups of humans

02/26/2022

Gears

I have become a man of gears.
Spur, Spiral Bevel, Hypoid even Nobokov
Racked by racks and rolled by Grobs.
I have traveled the world as an expert
On a subject that few people know or care about
Unless my expertise fails to work.
It is a perfect mesh of knowledge and uncaring
Need and ignorance

The machines:
Gleason, Klingelnberg, Mikron, Hoefler, Kapp, Mitsubishi
The list goes on and on
From Europe, the US, Japan, China, India, Korea
I have traveled this world to sell them,
To tell others how to use them
From Singapore aircraft plants with epoxy coated floors
To Indian forging plants with dirt floors
I have traveled
I have used my expertise

Solving problems of tooth spacing,
Hard line patterns in the roots of the teeth,
Heel patterns,
Toe patterns
High patterns
Low patterns
Split patterns
Adjusting eccentric angles
Changing feeds and speeds
Recalculating summaries
Reading scales

Exchanging my knowledge for money
My money for travel
My travel for culture
The Kuntz Haus in Zurich
A Tori Gate in Tokyo
The Blind Pig Barbecue in Tuscaloosa
Mercedes Benz in Gaggenau
Churrascaria in Brazil
Les Bateaux Mouches on the Seine

I am not guilty.
The gears made me do it…

12/26/2021

Inventory

This morning I am counting grinding wheels
Heavy, conical, blue ones glued to steel backing plates
Stocked on head high steel shelves, a chaos of random types.
I am wearing only one glove, the left glove
To protect my lifting hand from the abrasive grit
To leave the right hand free for writing
The roar of carburizing pits
The rumble of fork lifts
Distract me so I have to count some shelves two or three times.
And the blast of heat from a furnace door opening
Finds my face and my right hand
Sweating from the face mask and shield I work doggedly
Without pausing for rest or water
Wheels grinding, gears turning
Gears that keep turning in my head
Taking me back fifty years to sweeping the floor
In the filthy old shop on Chicago's west side
Under the El tracks
Across the street from
The Blessed Knee Walker Missionary Baptist Church
Down the street from Brach's Candy Company
The company that turned Mondays into butterscotch
Tuesdays into peppermint.
Today would be black cherry day and tomorrow lemon drop.

We all can hope for our days to come with a sweet smell
And not be filled with flames from the furnaces of hell.

02/08/2022

ZF

Early morning
And I am walking in a gear plant
Walking carefully
Walking on painted paths.
Paths with different colors
For different destinations
For different purposes
Some yellow paths
Join the red paths
Later to diverge
Or perhaps to join yet a green path.
I am counting grinding wheels
Grinding wheels for grinding hypoid gear teeth.
Rack upon rack of grinding wheels
And boxes full of grinding wheels
Passing rack upon rack of hypoid gears and pinions
Workers that I pass are all looking down,
Down at the colored paths
Or perhaps at their feet walking on the colored paths
All around are the sights and sounds of manufacturing
The hiss of air cylinders
The roar of furnace doors opening
The warning beeps of passing fork trucks
But these things must not distract me
I am counting grinding wheels,

And if I lose my place in the counting
I must return to the beginning
Back up the yellow path to begin again.

05/09/2022

Gilroy

Between high school and college
I lived for a time in the garlic capitol of the world.
Working in the petunia fields with
Jimmy and Raul and Sam
Jimmy the plant breeder,
And Raul the laborer,
And Sam the owner
And me the all around flunky.
Living in the Jensen hotel for nine dollars a week
In a room that had an iron bed that sagged in the middle
And a straight-backed chair with a wicker bottom
And a large iron safe to which I had no combination.
A strange combination of things for a bedroom
The bathroom down the hall
And a full on crazy neighbor, Don
Who stopped by at odd hours with tall tales of the CIA
And some foreign countries of which I had not heard.
A strange combination

But Gilroy was famous for garlic and the Wild One
With Brando riding his Harley with the trophy on the headlight
And the gang of bikers running wild in the town.
Gilroy stands atop the San Andreas Fault
Not my fault, or that of my crazy friend Don
Or my boss Raul
Or Jimmy the plant breeder
And I awoke each morning with the aroma of garlic in my nose
Garlic and sweat and the vague iron smell
Of the safe to which I had no combination.
After I went off to college, the fault gave way,
Splitting the town in two
After a strange combination
Of garlic and Harleys and petunias and tall tales of the CIA.

Maybe it was my fault after all.

06/20/2022

Antikythera

Clever those ancient Greeks.
They made a device found in an ancient shipwreck
Made back before year Zero
The device in an ancient shipwreck
Near the island of Antikythera archaeologists found
The device in a shipwreck
A device that mimicked the motion of celestial bodies
In our solar system.
Designed by amateurs without telescopes or computers Looking
    up from our planet, naked eyed
Planets, comets, and our sun mimicked by a gear train
A complicated train of bronze gears and shafts
Engineered jewelry, engineered art
Mechanical astronomy from the time of Christ
In a two thousand year old ship wreck
Analyzed by MRI's and CT scans
Analyzed by archaeologists and engineers and artists
With the tools of scientists—lasers and radiation
The Antikythera has not yet been analyzed enough.
Two thousand year old technology
And our superior science and technology
Have yet to figure out how it worked
And exactly what it did
How those primitives engineered and built
This wonderfully primitive futuristic device.

Did it precisely calculate the motions of the planets?
Or precisely track comets and distant galaxies,
Or maybe calculate a little prince's birthday?
Perhaps tell the dates of butterfly migrations.
We just don't know.
And not knowing is one of our best things.
The best things we hate the most about being human.

02/02/2022

71

Combat

In the Roman Coliseum gladiators pleased the masses
By killing and maiming each other
And assorted Tigers, Lions, Alligators, and Hippos.
The crowds went wild with vicarious violence.

Pits for dog fighting in the city of Detroit
Draw crowds of bloodthirsty bettors.

Bullfights on Crete and in Spain and Mexico
Yield celebrations of matadors as heroes, celebrities

In Poland, Germany
Jousting knights thrilled crowds of peasants and royalty

We are violent creatures. We pay butchers
To kill our meat for us while
We pay soldiers to kill our enemies

And here I sit watching Battlebots.
Rooting for "Rusty" the homemade barn born robot
Virtual Violence, robot gladiators of the future,
The Battlebots take the field to shouts of Fight! Fight! Fight!
Excited by the mechanized violence
I sit here in front of my television
Excited yet ashamed of it.

03/18/2022

My List

I made a list this week
Of all the human butchers that I thought were really bad.
I didn't know what the list was for but I made it anyway.
Started off with Joe Stalin—a proper choice
Continued with Idi Amin—a righteous butcher
Can't forget old Hitler and I
Later graced it with Michigan's own George Custer
Couldn't leave out Mao Zedong
And went back to Hernan Cortes
Not to mention Vladimir Putin.
Any road, I was feeling like I missed someone important
Until my pal Lee filled in the rest
By saying that these guys were bad asses
But none compared to one of his relatives.
Lee made me realize who I forgot.
All the women.
So I've been thinking.
We've got the odd female serial killer
An Egyptian female Pharoah
A flame haired warrior queen in England
And some Romanian Duchess who killed her servants
So she could bathe in their blood.
But none of these live up to the term Mass Murderer
Like even challenging the murderings
Of George Armstrong Custer.
Women had better step up their game.
This is the age of equality.

03/19/2022

tiny

I know, I know, I know,
we all think we are powerful, woke
we are harnessing the power of goodness
but we are smaller than quarks
with all the power of a fart in a hurricane

rulers feel the power of their guns
rulers feel the power of their bombs
bad guys can perpetuate war
we cannot touch them
with our prayers and mumbo jumbo
we are the good guys
the powerless.

but the bad guys are powerless as well.
while they feel powerful they have nothing
even if they are as big as a galaxy
as deep as the Marianas trench
they do not realize that

the universe will continue to snicker behind all of our backs.

04/16/2022

Wordless

I am wordless
Empty
The world has
Robbed me
Of them.
For a while
I thought
Writer's block
But I know better
I cannot express
My lonely terror
For my children
My grandchildren or
The people I
Do
Not
Know.
It is the
World
That miserable
Word Thief
My poems are dying of terrible times

04/22/2022

Peace

Forty thousand years ago
A cave with a family inside
A mother, a child, a hunter, animal skins to sleep on.
Hunter supplied food
Mother gathered the odd vegetable or grain.
Mother fed and cared for the child and
They slept together on the animal skins.

> Greed

Once on a hunting trip
The hunter noticed another cave, larger,
With a stream flowing along side
And he saw a mother and two children
Enjoying the sun on the soft grass in front by the stream,
Listening to the song of the stream.
Saw the other hunter bring home a fat grouse for dinner.

> Death

The first hunter waited one day
Until the other man had gone off to hunt for food.
When the other hunter was long gone
He slipped into the cave and killed the mother and both kids
With his club
A war crime
Forty thousand years ago.

> Tribes

Finally, a solution to the hunting and gathering
People gathered into groups to hunt and farm and work together.
Better groups, better society.
Better weapons, better killing,

Our crimes of war are now so perfected
That   I am too sad to go on.
Too scared to go on.
Too angry to go on.

I want to write our current state of nuclear war crimes
But I am too scared to go on.
I take this personally

I am scared to go on and I am too pissed off.
I'm so angry that I want to kick somebody's ass.
Too ANGRY to go on.
Maybe I'll just go ahead and kick somebody's ass.
War is my human right
My heritage.
We care more about the price of gasoline
We care more about getting a new car
We care more about our toenails
Than we do about a real solution.
Perhaps the death of all of our kind is the solution.
Let the cockroaches have the stupid planet after all.

04/29/2022

Miss Pope

I remember Miss Pope
Tall
Imposing
I remember See Jane and Michael and Spot the dog.
I remember two carrots plus one carrot equals three carrots.
I remember Miss Pope coming to my house for dinner
Invited by the parents.
I still remember her pulling into the drive
At the big old stucco house on Garfield Street
In her green '49 Ford convertible.
I do not remember dinner
Or the discussion
Until Miss Pope told our little group that she
Drove stock cars at Santa Fe Speedway.
The term Show Stopper does not begin to describe
What Miss Pope said.
My parents were politely disturbed.
But I was in love.

04/10/2022

Sanctuary of Knowledge

I walk slowly up the worn and marble steps
And swing the white and tall door open.
I step into the shadows of the ante room
The marble floor is black with silver veins
And my timid high school footsteps echo softly in the gloom.
The ceiling in this room, thirty feet high
Supported in the corners by white and Corinthian columns.
Lincoln and Jefferson gaze down at me from tall pedestals.
Judging me for frivolous use of this serious facility.

More white and tall doors swing to almost blinding light
And slowly, timidly I venture through
To walk between the rows of tall and wooden shelves.
Tall and wooden shelves of knowledge.
Long and sturdy tables and chairs for the knowledgeable
The silence is only broken by an infrequent cough
Or the squeak of chair legs on polished tiles.

I can feel the knowledge
Smell the slightly mildewed, welcoming pages
Of knowledge.
Breathe the paper and ink and leather covered knowledge
Stark black on faded linen pages or ancient maps
Or newspapers on strange and wooden spears.
Card catalogs and desks and tables of maple and oak,
Pine or plywood or steel are nowhere in this sanctuary.
These words and pictures and maps and drawings are
Organized and cataloged and preserved for all to share.
Yet I came to this sanctuary to get out of my house,
A house where my parents were oppressively stuffy,
Always talking of the past, of poetry and art and music.
A house filled with books and musical instruments
When I knew what was important:

Girls and football, motorcycles and fast cars.
Girls who always failed to notice me,
Football which I was too fat and slow to play
Motorcycles which I was forbidden to consider
And fast cars which I could never hope to afford.

These sanctuaries of knowledge are endangered today.
Wikipedia and Google are pushing card catalogs
And reference librarians onto the junk pile of history.
Our libraries have glowing terminals where
Hardwood card catalogs once glowed with maple colors
The maple book shelves have turned to steel.
Even the microfiche and
Newspapers on wooden spears gone
All in the cloud somewhere
And high school kids escape their ignorant parents
On Google or Instagram or some other screeny place.

And here I sit, lamenting the passing of libraries,
When all my wasted youth I used them to escape the house
Even when I had a faculty carrel in the stacks at University
I used it more to eat my lunch and to escape the students.

I would give a lot
Which I don't got
To have those years back so that then
I could abuse libraries yet again.

01/15/2022

Caitlin's Birthday

With Caitlin's birthday party part of history
We'd come at last exhausted with her packages
To home and bed.
But something still was buzzing in my head.
The cat was scratching on that ragged velvet chair when I arose.
Avoiding creaky steps I made my timid way into the kitchen.
The pale refrigerator stood there mocking by the arch
Two am and awfully late for me with a factory to open up at seven.

Her birthday morning crept in quietly as ice.
Excited, insomniacal I sat bare legged on the couch and thought
A soft electric motor keeping time
Answered by a numb and chiming silence
Paging through a book suggesting we send music to the stars.
Jill Tarter's dishes in wild Idaho blasting concerti skyward,
To let others know we're here.

But the schitzophrenic discussion: Mussorgsky or the Bee Gees
Could not recenter my restless brain.
For days I'd stood beside the Gleasons trying to quiet my mind
Various poems started up, began to flourish and died
Beside this rolling cradle and these reciprocating tools
Beside the involutes, pressure angles and concave curvatures
Somehow this poem made it all the way to her birthday
It rings as bell clear as a wine glass at a wedding
Caitlin's birthday is more than special to us.
Suddenly we are stumbling down the path of life
As three instead of two
Six feet confuse the way
Of this journey of discovery and loss
But we are better now and better will become
Anon

08/04/1978

81

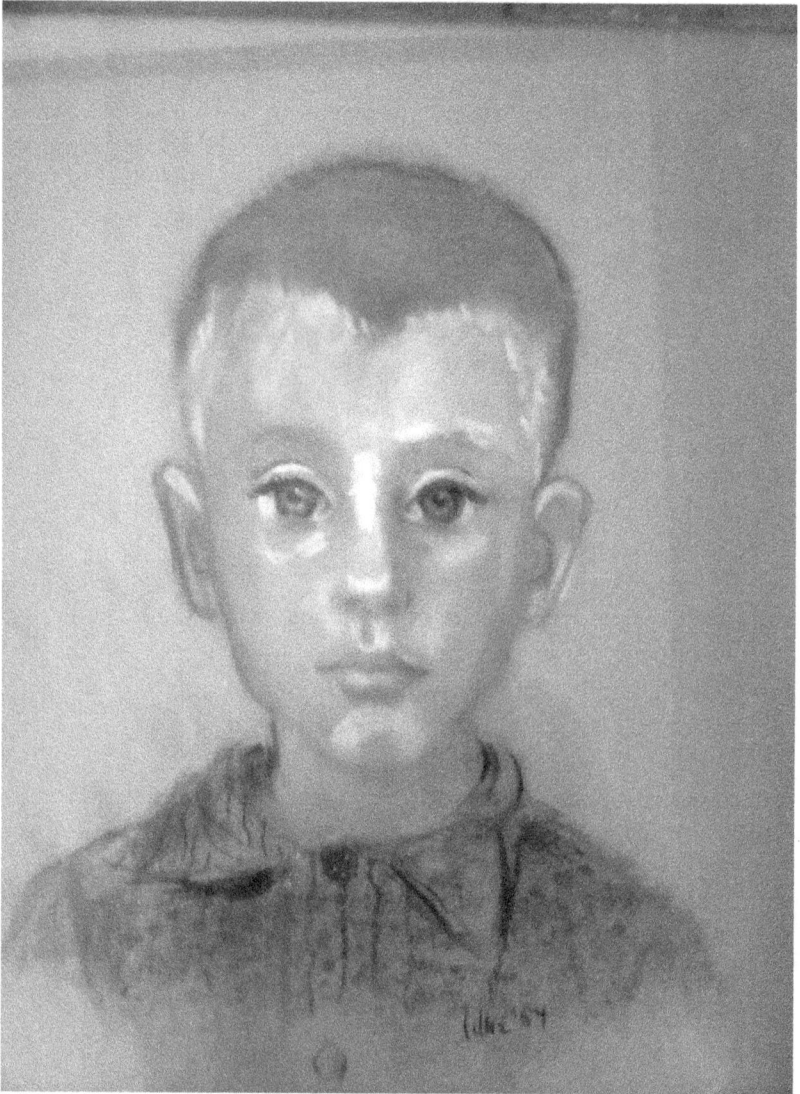

Transitions

Arthur Harjula's old yellow Piper Cub
Dropped onto the rocky air strip
Like a dirty sock into a hamper.
He rolled up to the head of the strip and turned around
Ready to head back to Thomaston and shut her down.
At ten, I was thrilled to see the old airplane
Thrilled to run over and greet whatever rich people
Had chosen to charter Arthur's old and rickety airship
To fly across Penobscot Bay to our old and rocky island.

Arthur had already climbed out
And stopped me from coming closer to the old Cub.
Danny, you run over to Harold Bunker's and tell him
That I need him to come over here right away.
I ran.
Responsibility a pretty proud thing to a ten year old.
Harold put me in his old Jeep
And bounced the quarter mile back to the airstrip
The airstrip that was once a good potato field
Behind our big old farmhouse
On Matinicus Island in the North Atlantic
That once sustained a tribe of Penobscot Indians
The airstrip that my family bought with the old farm
And now was home to all us summer people
On an island in transition
Transition from lobster fishing to tourism.
Arthur waited by the old yellow Cub
His passenger's head leaning back
Arthur and Harold shooed me back home
Not wanting me at ten to know that I had seen a corpse.
Her transition had happened in the air over the ocean
Ours are yet to come
Somewhere

12/14/2021

83

Fletcher

You lay there:
Hospitalized
Dying
Hallucinating
Not even knowing it was me.
Barely conscious
Your hands tied to the bed and
You were belted to the bed.
And I was reading Lewis Thomas' Lives of a Cell
A kind of ironic choice I now see;
But his wise philosophical and biomedical prose soothed me
Soothing the reader not the listener
Captive audience
Tied to a bed.
The words allowing me to escape temporarily
From your fate and my own
To escape the sight, the smell, the smell of bleach, ammonia
And death

01/20/22

Death by Zoom

We thought the eyes were windows to the soul
But now we all have other windows.
My family is meeting on Zoom
Our brother Ted is dying
A complication of older cousin, stepbrother
He is dying of cancer in North Carolina
Choosing to opt out of treatment
Choosing the quality of life of morphine
And we gather at our latest window to his soul
Zoom.
Ted, Carol and their kids,
Shelley, Nancy, Lee and I are wanting to see into his soul
But by staring so hard into his soul we fail to notice
That he can see right back into ours.
Every stupid joke
Every poor proposal
Every clumsy statement
Flies through the zoom eye and bounces back into all of us.
Unseen his zoom eyes
Bounce into all of us.
It is a window with eight way glass.

05/25/2022

Billy Snapp

Learning disabled
Fetal alcohol syndrome
Only thirteen when he died
Of desire, or love, or lust, or telephone
He confessed his interest in a girl at junior high
And his mother told him to call her.
His error was listening to his mother
Who had put his brain in that condition in the first place.
The girl said she wasn't allowed to go out with anyone.
Rejected by her, he killed himself.
That'll teach 'em

05/24/2022

Vermont

In Paradox, New York the road rises,
Becoming a majestic arch crossing the lake
To the rapids at Winooski
To ones that I love
And I am limited to carefully chosen words
Carefully regulated subjects
Brittle tiptoeing brunch at the rapids with passion and apathy
To the coop grocery
To the maple syrup creamy store
To the lumber mill
Evenings reading at some cheap motel.
Family pulled in many ways by human moods, and prejudice,
Family, a sometimes caustic mix that we cannot avoid
Family a magnet to which we are drawn again and again.
And then it's arching over the lake again to Paradox
Through the Adirondacks
And back to Michigan.
Back to ones I love
Back to words of carefully crafted poetry
Back to alone
Back to lonely.

08/17/2004

Weather

Why are we, the old people
So damned obsessed by weather?
If I have heard the weather report six times
On any given morning before breakfast
I cannot leave the room if it comes on again.
If this season gives us hot, hot it will be.
Rain? It will be wet.
Snow? It will be cold
Knowing cannot change it.
Yet I listen to the Oracle at TV
Like some Greek acolyte at Delphi.
I even email friends in Italy and Japan about it
Odd this being old
Odd this change in the world climate

04/19/2021

Vegan

So here I am
A vegan old guy with my ass in the chair
Watching television
Getting excited by none other than Gordon Ramsey
Who is killing his own antelope to eat in Romania
And Wicked Tuna is hauling huge
And sleek and lovely fish into their boat
And the Deadliest Catch is hauling in king crab by the ton

I am fascinated by scenes of animal harvesting
Mostly, I think because I used to do it.
And now, since I was encouraged by my doctor to be vegan
I have become one of those people I used to laugh at
Putting spiders alive out in the back yard,
And using the have a heart trap on the mice.
Amazing myself by calmly watching while
A centipede crosses the room
And disappears into a crack in the baseboard.
And when I stand watching the skunk that lives in the backyard

I no longer even miss the taste of lobster
Although I've eaten thousands of them growing up in Maine.
I no longer miss beef tenderloin
Although I lived so many years in Illinois.
I'm just vegan
Vegan with benefits

03/17/2022

Fog

Cool grey blanket
Softening the world
Distancing sensations
Fog has a cool feel
A scent of mystery
Out of the fog ghostly islands appear,
Their rocky coasts with spruce trees indistinct.
Ledges suddenly break out of the curtain of grey ocean
I can smell land in the fog
I can smell fish in the fog
I can feel exhaustion in the fog
I can feel hunger in the fog
I can feel going home with lobsters for dinner in the fog.
I can feel the dampness in my boots in the fog.
Fog softens the world, making it fecund, damp, growing
Fog makes us move more slowly,
Fog makes us listen more carefully
Fog has a roll over and stay in bed feeling
Fog has a hide from the world feeling
Fog makes us feel like gathering together

The fog of war makes terror appear suddenly
The fog of war is made from particles of blood and tissues
The fog of war is made of sadness
The fog of war is made of us
The fog of war, a part of humankind from our beginning.
The fog of war will be our end.

03/02/2022

The Color of Water

Blue as the ocean, we are rumbling out of the harbor,
Past the grey granite breakwater.
And I look down the golden path of fire to the sun.
And turning to look astern see the foam of our wake
Spread out like a Delta of white
Richard and I stand on the slippery deck
In yellow oilskins, yellow Sou'westers, yellow jackets
Looking through pilot house windows for orange buoys
Avoiding other colored buoys
Avoiding other lobstermen's traps
Looking over the red foredeck to the blue ocean

Slowing to pick up our first buoy,
I sense movement to starboard
And glancing over I see grey porpoises jumping
Grey porpoises rolling in our wake, playing in the white.
Grey as concrete, smooth as mercury
They play while we work
We work while they live their porpoise lives, playing.

We work together on the water
Water that is colorless water that is clear
But we never work out our red and blue differences.
They pollute these waters, aquatic politics
Twisting, swirling, yet almost always separate
Never purple, never coming together

It's been the human way for fifty thousand years
As natural as sunrise
We kill each other's tribes
We kill to have more things
Bigger houses
Bigger boats

More land
But mostly we kill for power...

And politics are power.
We kill for colors

03/02/22

Matinicus Church

It stands
Faded dark blue flaking paint baked by the sun,
Assaulted by the fog most mornings,
A single pointed bell tower reaching heavenward.

Mom played the old pump organ for the Sunday crowd of Fifty
    fishermen and wives and children
Who complained to themselves that she
Played the old pump organ too fast
"The Old Rugged Cross" and "In the Garden" too fast
While a sixties hippie looking Jesus looked on,
Saintly, quiet smile on his stained glass lips.

At a Christmas long ago, I was natural bearded Santa
For the Island folk at this old church,
Giving out gifts to the fishermen and wives and kids.
Candy and books and gag gifts, like a peanut butter boat
Repair kit for Albert and a custard pie for me.

And in summer the Church supper was a huge event.
Rhubarb jam and homemade sweet rolls for sale
Before we all set down (you don't sit down here)
To a dinner of lobster salad, mac and cheese and pop.
No booze in the church (that was outside the back door)
We tough lobstermen drank outside the door, while
Jesus looked piously toward the setting sun
As we all patted rounded bellies.

And we all headed home to get a good night's rest
Before going out to haul in the morning.
I helped Aunt Marion into Cliff Young's ancient Chevy
And hopped into the back, sitting on the side rail
And we dodged pot holes on the old gravel road

For half a mile to her ancient house
As I hold on to my rhubarb pie for dear dessert.

Mom and Dad walked all the way and got home
Before old Cliff Young bounces the ancient Chevy
Up to the dooryard of our old white house
To let me get some sleep before we go to haul
In the morning at sunrise.

As Jesus smiles his enigmatic smile
And my mind repeats
"Let the Lower Lights Be Burning
Send a beam across the waves"
As we head on a bright orange path into the sun.
Out to haul in the morning
Early

12/12/21

Sleeping on the Twine

It's been a long night of chasing herring
Without a moon, the calm and peaceful ocean is almost spooky
But as the sky in the East begins to brighten,
We head home, a couple of hours west,
And I collapse onto the pile of dripping twine
Aurora Borealis has long since faded
Along with the phosphorescent glow of plankton in the water
Along with the brightening in the east
Along with our determination to set twine again.
I lie there savoring the rumble of the diesel
And fall fast asleep
Until we round the head of the breakwater
In full sunrise we bump the wharf
And I head up the road to home
For a breakfast of fresh caught herring slivers
And some of the mackerel
That were here and there among the herring
The flashing silver and the black and blue stripes
Blending into a living palate of breakfast
As they were pumped aboard our living breakfast
All of the crew grabbed some to take for breakfast.
Tonight we rinse and repeat.
Time passes as do we,
Indeed

05/25/2022

Neil and the Crow

A big black bird
Is pecking at some flat and rotting carcass
On the yellow line in the middle of this country road.
And as I slow to avoid it
It hops, unconcerned, to the other side
Never missing a peck at the
Flattened, rotting mess for another tasty morsel.
Keeping one eye on the car
It continues pecking, peeking

And as I straighten out and drive around a curve
My mind twists back to mythology
The Giant Prometheus chained, with a crow pecking
At his liver by day and
His liver growing back at night.
Punished by the gods for loving humans
For caring, for bringing them fire for warmth.
A curious organ, the liver, growing back for Prometheus
As it does for humans.
My pal has liver cancer and doctors just cut
The cancer out.
The healthy part is growing back.
Curious, Human, Caring

12/08/2021

Send in the Clowns

We set our traps in a giant circle around Matinicus Rock.
Baren, uninhabited, with only a lighthouse
As a sign of civilization
Gulls, gilamonts, cormorants, wild geese and ducks
Swirled
Honked
Screeched
All around our boat as we hauled our traps.
An occasional whale and many porpoises rolled
But the best moment
The moment to remember
Was when the puffins came back to the island
With little fish in their beaks to feed their young.
Streaking along, barely clearing the wave tips
They made no sound.
They had one job
But their appearance Clowns of the Air
Said it all.
Said it best
Parenting: There ought to be Clowns

3/22/2022

The Code of Divorce

Hammurabi lay down the laws
Two hundred eighty-two of them cuneiform chiseled
On a black stone stele in the marketplace of Babylon.

You, of course had many more,
Unwritten
Unspoken
Only in your mind
But I sure found out when I managed to violate some of them.
How could I not know that my black leather jacket
With all the zippered pockets and my favorite patches
Should never hang in the entry way closet?
Or that the outside patio chairs had to be in a perfect U shape
With only the red cushions toward the door window?
Or that the carpet had to be vacuumed in a certain pattern?
The preferred was herringbone; but parallel lines permitted
My car had to be clean and empty of discarded coffee cups,
While yours looked like an Alabama alley after a tornado.
Hammurabi was an eye for an eye kinda king.
You were an eye for an eye lash kinda queen
His law demanded a tooth for a tooth
But yours demanded a tooth for a tooth brush.
Do I sound bitter?
You bet your ass I do
Because I am.

02/07/2022

Quintero

Stop on the Underground Railroad
Between Missouri a slave state and Nevada the free one
Separated by the Mississippi River
Separated by misery and muddy death
Now a city excavated like Pompei
By archaeologists who dig with paintbrushes
Painstakingly recovering cornerstones
And pottery and abandoned homesites.

The town was built in 1857
The same year Iddo Tolman
Built the old frame house on Matinicus Island, Maine
There were no slaves involved in Iddo's house
Just a lot of wives.
Iddo had thirteen children
But only three wives
On that rocky little island in Maine.
But the rocky little island yielded potatoes

And now Quintero yields up its' hidden secrets
For slavery and ignorance and hatred
For human failings.
A hidden shame
We're all to blame.

06/20/2022

Young King Tut

I am twelve
And Mister Ferguson, just a block away
From the old stucco house on Garfield Street
In a one story brick with a funny steel tower on the roof
Thought he could be a mentor to a local kid and
He asked me if I would like to see something interesting
And I said "Sure"
And followed him down to his basement.
When he flipped on the light, the glowing tubes
Flourescent tubes
Weird buzzing tubes
Lit the room with blueish vibrating light
The room that was filled with strange electronic gear
And on the wall above the microphone on the desk was
W9YKT.
I was hooked into ham radio and followed the hobby for years.

Today, if someone invited my twelve year old grandson
To come down to his basement to see his video game system
My pervert radar would go off like a bomb.
But that was 1959 and now is now.
And I learned a lot from that old man
About radio and being mentored in a strange electric basement
With the call sign K nine Young King Tut

06/21/2022

Stalker

Suddenly I understand the stalkers of the world.
That woman at the counter of the bakery
Is so strangely attractive that I have come back
Repeatedly to see her smile when I bought
A loaf of rye, or was it wry?
Or came in for a pretty lousy sandwich
Two days in a row.
I even made sure my clothes were clean
My shirt tucked in properly
My goddamned hair combed.
The bakery isn't very close
Nor is it the best in town,
Yet her quirky looks and just plain attitude
Keep bringing me back.

You don't understand
I don't want to date her
Or marry her
Or get with her at all.
I don't understand either
I still can't understand

She talks and flirts and smiles
And puts a special cookie on the plate
With the pretty lousy sandwich
And after another trip for lunch I notice
Other old guys who have come in for the same
Exclusive treatment.
Funny that I didn't notice them before.
I wonder if they are dressed as well as me
Or if they drive as nice a car as I do.
And I realize that by cracky I am jealously guarding
This woman as if I have some rights to her affections

Not only do I have no rights to her affections
I don't even want them.

05/06/2022

Holy Land USA

There were five of us
Five of us college bums and three dogs
And snacks and luggage
And guitars in the sixty-three Bonneville wagon
And the car top carrier
Between Illinois and Maine
And did I mention three dogs?
Needing a spot for a picnic lunch
We pulled off in Pennsylvania
A rustic looking road that wound around a hill into thick woods
And above our picnic ground, a huge cross
And the words Holy Land USA on the top of the hill.
Holy Land indeed,
Dogs ran free and we lunched in the shadow of the cross.

And on to complete the trip to Rockland, Maine
To catch the old slow ferry boat to Matinicus
To invade my parent's house on the isolated island.

We fished, and chopped down spruces and swatted mosquitos
Sleeping in the old attic of the old farm house
For two weeks of glorious freedom and freedom and fun.
Eating lobster and codfish and wrinkles and pollack
And picking wild strawberries so Mom could make pies.
It was, indeed Holy Land USA.

07/16/2022

Poetic License

I have been pulled over by the verse police
And when I manage to find my poetic license
The cop sees that it's expired.
I have been writing on an expired license for years.
What will be the sentence?
Will it be rhyme jail?
The stony lonesome of words?
The grey meter hotel?
The poetic penitentiary?
Alas I know where I will go.
The Writer's Block.

07/23/2022

Haiku 235

We have plenty of
Uranium Two, Three, Five
To make peace on Earth

Haiku 505

Leave Bigfoot alone
What did he do already
Fuck your sister's dog?

Haiku Gruntled

I am gruntled and
Mayed, hinged, fuddled by my own
Small humanity

Haiku At Matinicus Church

Aunt Marion smells
A geranium leaf and
Looks at the Jesus window

Haiku Living

We suffer from
The terminal disease that
Is known as living

Haiku for Milt

My father's hands are
In front of me to steer the
Car, to hold the pen

02/15/2022

Message in a Bottle

Daddy, I was seven
And we were staying at the big cottage on the West Side
And you took me out on cold mornings
When the rest of the family was sleeping
And we walked the rock beach to Little Island at low tide
Discovering tide pools
Finding surprises like that huge red jellyfish
Slipping on the smooth rocks
The kelp covered smooth rocks.
I thought you were showing me the wonders of the ocean
And spending special time with just me.
I didn't realize until I was a parent
That you were sparing mom and Nancy from
My irritating, overactive presence.

Daddy was being good to the family
To me.
And he showed me the tradition of sending a note in a bottle
Casting my words out into the ocean
For someone to find and wonder about my words
Albeit a continent away
A beginning of my poems,
A tweet of the nineteen fifties
Foreshadowing of this poem
Foreshadowing of this culture
This world

08/13/2022

About the Author
Daniel Webster Carleton

Dan has been a father, a brother, a family member. His two adult children, Ace and Jordan both have followed in his footsteps and each runs his own business. Working as a machinist, a lobster fisherman, and a salesman he has managed to support himself for the last sixty years.

He taught poetry at the University of Illinois in Urbana, Illinois in the 1960's. Dan's mom, Frances Griffith Carleton encouraged him to write poetry from an early age and he never succeeded in breaking the habit.